The story Begins
AF448462

In a quiet corner of the forest, a little rabbit gazed out from her burrow, dreaming of a world beyond the trees.

One day, the rabbit gathered her courage and stepped outside. Today was the day she would explore the unknown.

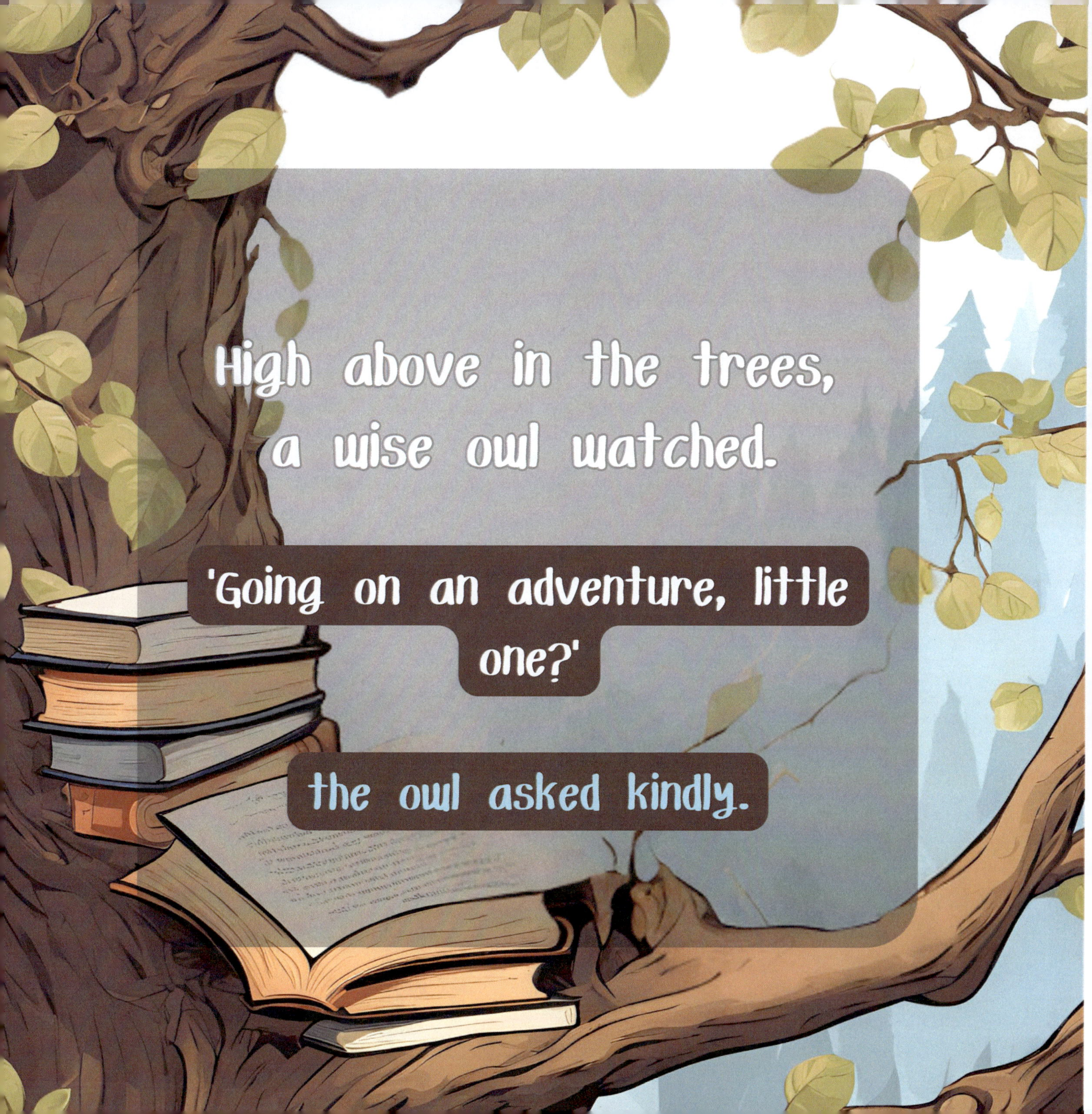
High above in the trees, a wise owl watched.
'Going on an adventure, little one?"
the owl asked kindly.

'Every adventure needs knowledge,'

said the owl.

'Here, take this book. It will guide you.'

The rabbit smiled and thanked her new friend.

With the book hold in her
arm, the rabbit set off.
The forest seemed bigger
than she imagined, but
she felt ready.

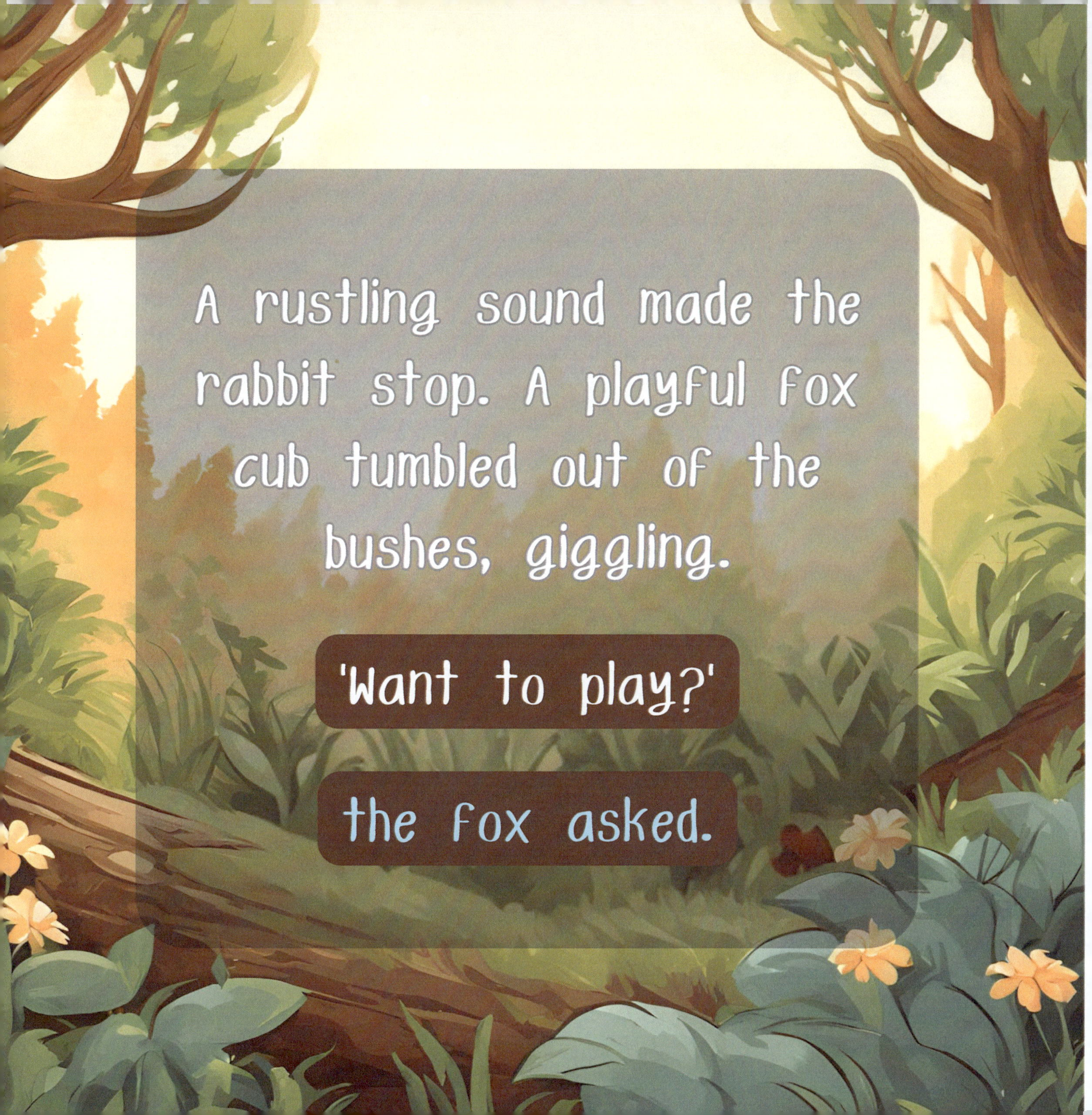

A rustling sound made the rabbit stop. A playful fox cub tumbled out of the bushes, giggling.
'Want to play?'
the fox asked.

'Let's play a game,'
said the fox.
'If you win, I'll tell you the secret to being quick and clever.'

After thinking hard, the rabbit solved the fox's puzzle.

The fox cheered,

'You did it! Now you know—being clever is as important as being brave.'

Now the fox and the
rabbit walked together.
The forest became
thicker, but the rabbit
felt confident with a
friend by her side.

Soon, they reached a
peaceful meadow filled
with flowers. A
graceful deer appeared,
her antlers adorned
with a crown of
blossoms.

'Kindness is the greatest strength,'
said the deer.
'Helping others makes you truly brave.'
She gently showed the rabbit how to care for the flowers.

The rabbit thanked the deer for her wisdom. With a heart full of kindness, the rabbit and fox continued their journey.

The trees grew tall and dark as the friends entered a shadowy part of the forest. The rabbit felt a shiver of fear.

Out of the shadows stepped a silver wolf with glowing eyes.
'Don't be afraid,'
the wolf said gently.
'I'm here to help.'

The wolf smiled.
'Courage is not the absence of fear,'
she said,
'But doing what's right even when you're scared.'

They soon came upon a fallen tree blocking their way.
'Together, we can move this,'
said the wolf.
'You are stronger than you think.'

With their combined strength, they moved the tree. The rabbit smiled, realizing she was braver and stronger than she knew.

They rested under the stars, gazing at the twinkling sky.

'You've learned so much,' said the wolf. 'You should be proud.'

The next morning, the rabbit felt a new sense of strength. She knew she was ready for any challenge that lay ahead.

They reached the top of a small hill, where the whole forest stretched out below them. It was more beautiful than the rabbit ever imagined.

The rabbit smiled, thinking
of the friends she had met
and the lessons she had
learned about bravery,
cleverness, and kindness.

'We should help others in the forest,'
said the rabbit.
'Let's share what we've learned!'
The others agreed enthusiastically.

The trio encountered a lost squirrel.

'Can you help me find my way home?'

the squirrel asked, looking worried.

Using their cleverness, kindness, and courage, they guided the squirrel back to its home, teaching it how to be brave.

The squirrel was grateful.
'Thank you for helping me!'
it squeaked.
'I'll always remember your kindness!'

The friends continued on,
spreading kindness
throughout the forest.
Each creature they met
felt the warmth of
friendship.

Word spread through the forest. Animals gathered to celebrate the friendship that had blossomed among them.

'Together, we are stronger!'

said the rabbit.

All the animals cheered, understanding the strength of unity and kindness.

And so, the rabbit learned that adventure is not just about exploring new places but also about sharing kindness and courage.

At the end of every adventure lies the heart of kindness, courage, and friendship—lessons that last forever.

* 9 7 8 9 8 4 3 6 0 3 9 7 5 *